Poems

Of

Cats & Dogs

Poems of Cats & Dogs; An Anthology
Copyright © 2023 Compiled by Pat Fogarty
Granite Publishing

ISBN: 978-1-950105-46-5
HB 1551065906
Printed in the USA

Dedication

This Book of Cat and Dog Poems is dedicated to all the kind souls who treat their pets with the love, care, and the respect our pets truly deserve.

I would also like to include in this dedication those special pet owners who adopted a cat or dog from one of those great organizations that rescue abandoned and stray animals.

And finally, I would especially like to honor and include in this dedication those kind folks and organizations who work with finding homes for abandoned or lost animals. People like Frank Bosco, who you'll get to know more about as you read some of his poems about a feral cat that was trapped under the Boardwalk in Atlantic City and brought to the county's animal shelter.

Roy Boy, the feral cat Frank eventually adopted is a heartfelt story in itself. But, the time and effort Frank as a volunteer working with his local *Petsmart* put into finding a home for this feral cat is also an amazing story, which may become a heartwrenching and heartfelt story in a future publication.

Preface

Sharing the love pet owners across the USA have for their pets became the driving force behind this collection; *Poems of Cats & Dogs*. The decision to include a photo of the pet of the poet was an easy one. Most of the poets whose work you will see in this collection include the displaying of their pets with their poems. Several of our poets wrote wonderful poems about long-gone pets from their childhood years. And because some of these pets crossed over many years ago, they did not have a photo of their pet. Such is life. We are not always able to carry the physical memories, such as photos, writings, and maybe even old 8 mm movies of our pets with us on our journey through the years. But as long as we have the memories of our pets, from no matter how long ago, we can still pay tribute to them by writing about them. As the submissions of poems started arriving for this collection; the number of tributes to pets that had crossed over the proverbial "Rainbow Bridge" dominated the field. Although I am not a psychology major, I realized my request for poems about Cats & Dogs became a healing tool for those still grieving the loss of a pet. If writing a poem can heal someone's sorrow, so be it. I am all for that. As you read many of these poems, you will come to see, without the kindness of the many people who adopted strays or otherwise unwanted cats & dogs from one of the thousands of animal rescue organizations across America, the outcome for the time these animals had in this world would not have been pleasant.

Table of Contents

Poems

of

Cats & Dogs

Laddie, Goodbye

You chose me when we first met.
As I sat on the breeder's couch, you climbed
into my arms, to never leave my side.
Our bond was sealed with mutual love.
You grew from a playful two-year-old
into a handsome Shetland Sheepdog.
A sable with classic collie splendor,
your beauty came from within and out.
Full of your own games, you herded
big dogs like they were your sheep.
You bounded carefree through snow
and barked when I opened pop-top cans.
Bold Lad, you were caring, kind, and true.
No one could resist your expressive eyes.
You adored your canine friends and
excelled in obedience school classes.
Then came the day, when you were nine,
the vet said sadly you had a failing heart.
How could that be? No dog ever had
a more perfect, purer heart or soul. Ever…
You persevered with wonder and delight,
even when your breathing slowed and
labored. You taught me how to live each

day of life as though it were my last.
One night, as you slept by my bed,
your golden heart stopped beating.
It broke our hearts to say goodbye,
but we know you are not at rest.
You have bounded over the Rainbow
Bridge to make new dog friends there.
And you're still in my heart every day.
I hear your bark and see your joyful eyes.
I know dogs go to Heaven. Why wouldn't they?
They possess beauty without vanity, strength
without insolence, courage without cruelty…
All of man's virtues without his vices.

Ω

© Sandy Nelson

The Opportunist

your age is written on your muzzle
how much time left, St. Francis' puzzle
we broke bread with friends
as such all must come to an end
so with hugs and kisses we sigh
we walk and say our goodbyes
so well behaved

we let you stay

so why when we return

don't we ever learn

we find you

no longer pining

happily dining

while

meandering across

the farmhouse table

who knew you were able

with St. Francis watching

and caring

he knew we wouldn't mind sharing

Ω

©Maureen Norcross

Pug Leo Portrait

You ignored repeated requests to pose
No response to my earnest pleas
Had to settle for hastily snapped photos
Close study and sketches (no fleas)

Onto canvas faint- penciled, browned
Outline of that mini- leonine mug; so,
Then terre verte as verdant surround
For tar-black muzzle and tawny torso

5

Eyes woeful dark, beady gaze up and out

At what? Meat morsel? Mistress' smile?

Shiny-lit nostril, foreshortened snout

Tongue protruded. Hangdog style

Tan torso with frontal white tuft

Forelimb displayed; claws retracted

Pacific, no bark; no manners sloughed.Ingredients

in place; no viewer distracted

Ω

©Ernest Griffith

Writing a Poem about Toby

If I could write a poem about my dog,

I would say he's been the greatest joy and best

friend in my life.

He's been the most unconditional loving partner

I've ever had.

If I could write a poem about my dog,

the words would shine,

the pen would be bright gold,

the paper would be the most expensive paper I

could buy.

If I could write a poem about my dog,

I'd hold it to my heart,

I'd kiss it gently,

and I'd put in on my altar

for the rest of my days.

Ω

©Kaya Kotzen

Lullaby for Puppy

When the sun is setting in Puppy Town,

Little puppies are turning round and round

To find the very best place to sleep,

To dream of bunnies and squirrels and sheep.

Tomorrow they'll greet a brand new day,

And little puppies will run and jump and play!

For there's nothing a puppy would rather be,

Then the very best friend to you and me!

Good night, little puppy!

Ω

©Mark Wenden

©Abbie by Shelley Lowell

The Last Line

If you were human
You'd be driving,
But your four legs,
No longer four-wheel drive,
And your four paws,
Slipping and sliding,
Still trying to chase felines,
Are failing with your body.

Your eyes meet mine
And I wonder if you remember
All the years and adventures
All the love and care from the start.
Your eyes seem to speak,
Though the interpretation is loose,
Your eyes, framed by gray,
Still young and kind at heart.

If you were human,
You'd be a centenarian,
With your walker or your cane,
Telling tall tales of long tails,
And exploring endless trails.
The good old days gone by
Are now sweet memories,
Yet clouded by your pain.

Will you see your long lost bro
On the other side?
Will you forgive me if it's time,
If it's your time to go?
Where are nurses
For lives like yours?
Why is the dreaded dead end
Eventually the only road?

Is it weird if I call you son
When your nursing home
Has been our home
And you're clearly a canine?
I'll just say "Good boy"
And rub your head
And struggle to write
The Last Line

Ω

©Jessica Lynn MacLean

©Gracie by Shelley Lowell

Roy Boy

Feline

Feral Unfriendly

Frightened Caged Confused

Cat Bowl Bars Blanket

Untrusting Sensitive Cute Adoptable

Persistent Patience

Adopted

Ω

©Frank Bosco

©Elwood by Shelley Lowell

Bird Watching in a Heat Wave

Jeffrey finds a cool spot in the shade
to watch the birds at feeders in the pear tree
juncos and towhees pecking at seeds
hummingbirds flitting around the sugar-water
jays squabbling over peanuts

His emerald eyes seem to stalk
but I'm pretty sure he's faking it. Look –
he's not crouched in attack mode, muscles tensed.
He's stretched out languid as a child just waking.
Even the birds aren't fooled

Jeffrey isn't mine – well, not anyone's really,

cats don't do submission. I mean to say I'm not
the one who feeds him.
But I have my uses. He rolls on his back and howls
till I scratch his belly, stroke his throat

Sufficiently adored
he hoists himself to the lip of the birdbath
ignoring the furious clamor of displaced birds
drinks deep
then curls up beneath a deck chair and falls asleep.

Ω

©*Marilyn Bowden*

Feral to Friend

The day we met

You were caged

The next day

You hissed at me

The next day

You showed your fangs

The next day

You ignored me

The next day

You yawned

The next day you

You meowed

The next day

You purred

The next day

I put food in your cage

The next day

You were waiting

The next day

You let me hold you

The next day

The same thing

The next day

They changed your sign

The next day

The sign cried out

Adult Cat

Seeking ForeverHome

The next day

I still came to you

The next day

Your eyes spoke

The next day

You spoke again

The next day

I told you

The next day

I filled out forms

The next day

The shelter called

The next day

I took you home

The next day

I named you

The Next day

You accepted your home

The next day

No longer mattered

The next day

You made your choice

The next day

You chose your human

The next day

And the next day

And the next day

And

The next day

For the next six years

Our friendship grew

From trepidation and fear

To respect and care

Every next day

Until the very end

I kept you warm

I kept you dry

I cared for you

I kept you healthy

I kept you nourished

And most of all

Roy Boy

I kept you loved

And loved and love and loved

Ω

©Frank Bosco

This Dumb Dog (Doug)

No one wanted this dumb dog
No one cared.

Dropped him over the fence
This dumb dog.

Unceremoniously abandoning him
Looked the other way.
Searching for others to own him
No one wanted him here.

Nobody stepped up to take him
This dumb dog.

Time passed by during the hunt
Warmth for him grew.

Twelve years flew, he has a home
This dumb dog.

Ω

©Elizabeth Ajamie-Boyer

A Soft Place

I shove the wheelbarrow
through the mud.
Brute strength, I think.
Wishing I had it.
Just – dig – the – hole.

Dig – the – hole,
Just – dig – the – hole.
My neighbor is out feeding
his horses and comes
over and stands by me, watching.

It's sleeting and raining.
Not hard, but enough to run like
rivulets of sweat down
my face, twining in my hair.

That shovel is too short,
my neighbor says. I say I know,
but I don't and wonder
what he means.
The mud is so heavy.

I won't let him have my short shovel,
though he offers. This is the last
bit of loving I can do.

I am so cold –
My coat is soddened with rain.
I raise a corner of the wet
quilt. He's sleeping,
curled up like a pup.

Just – dig – the – damn – hole.
One more shovelful.
The neighbor says it's deep enough
(coyotes wander through this field).
Ω

©Janet Hopkins

Theo and Jax

It was a cold and dry
December day
When our big boy Theo
Was called away

He was the cat
That adopted me
It was love at first sight
It was meant to be

He slept on my pillow
Every nite in our bed
A Davey Crockett raccoon cap
Encircling my head

Often times he'd put
His paw on my face
Letting me know
That he loved this place

Ω

©Mike Doyle

Stevie's Story

I was a Baltimore cat

every day before my human dad

left for work

he'd let me out to play

I roamed our city block

of old rowhouses

explored alleys

played with strays

chased birds

rats or an

occasional squirrel

I was lonely

My favorite part of the day was

29

when I spotted Sammy
walking his human mom
he was a black and white
Shih Tzu with big black soulful eyes

I love dogs

I loved my human dad's dog too
he'd let us play together
when he was home
which wasn't often

Sammy was the perfect size for me

When I saw them walking towards me
I'd hide behind a trash can, tree or steps
wait as they passed my hiding place
then I'd run up to Sammy
from behind and rub against him

Sammy didn't respond in kind
in fact he stiffened up
waiting for me to stop
I didn't care
I loved him

When I stopped
they'd continue on
I'd run up to him again
rub my face in his fur
rub my body against his
this went on until
we reached his rowhouse

This was my daily routine
for six months or more
no matter the weather
I was out there
waiting for Sammy
no matter the time of day
I was out there
waiting for Sammy
rubbing up against him
never tiring of this game

He was patient
always waiting until I stopped
he'd never bite or hurt me
A true gentleman!

One day I heard his mom
talking with a woman
hoping Sammy was there
my curious nature took over
I followed the sound of their voices
ending up in a backyard

Sadly, he was not there

His mom stopped talking
she went into the house
Maybe she's getting Sammy
I thought
I was so excited

She came out carrying a small box
with a door and handle
She opened its door while
placing it on the ground
I went inside thinking
Sammy might be in here

He wasn't

The door closed behind me

I was in the house

before I knew it

she opened the box's door

let me out

hugged me

kissed my head

petted me head to tail

just like mama cat used to do

She was very loving

very gentle

I liked that

no human ever hugged me

She said:

you are a handsome tuxedo cat

you are way too gentle and sweet

to be roaming these city streets

it's too dangerous for you

now you are an indoor cat

your name will be Stevie,

short for Stevia

because you are so sweet

That was fine with me

I could be with Sammy all day!

sleep next to him

eat with him

rub up against him

play with other cats here too

I felt very content

very safe

I wasn't lonely anymore

Ω

©Shelley Lowell

Annie

Oh Annie cat of tabby coat
your underside white mink
tiptoe by on pristine paws
concealing well-honed razor claws
your tongue and nose and footpads
a wash of gentle pink

Rounded form on compact legs
disguise your hunting prowess
lizards, mice, a robin once
fall to your deadly pounce
generous you share these treats
divided ounce for ounce

Shy of laps you reign supreme
on the sofa's padded arm
and revel in the stroking brush
at evening and at dawn

No, you say, *don't touch my head*
but here's my furry belly
leaving claws all safely sheathed
I'll soften into jelly
until you pull from under chair
my snake of braided leather

I'll stalk then pounce with lightning speed
that wiggling, tempting tether

When we get tired we go to bed
across my feet you spill
your years of sleeping out of doors
or sprawled upon a hard bare floor
are past, your dreams fulfilled

I miss your sweetness, little friend
still saddened by your sudden end
my tears now mixed with memory
with gladness that you came to me

Ω

Songwoman
©Sharon Seymour

Mia

Friend

Curious Courageous

Patrol Protect Pursue

Calm Care Comfort Company

Play Explore Defend

Precious Cherished

Remembered

©Pat Fogarty

©Corkey by Shelley Lowell

Lucky All Around

Silky soft to the touch and cuddly as down
With long ears that sweep all the way to the ground
With a coat of white splotched with taffy brown

I could warm a heart or bring a smile,
Or erase a bad day that began with a frown

My puppy antics could compete with
The silliest of clowns
Sometimes I trip over my own feet
And tumble down
Next time it's my ears
And down I go round and round

When it was time for a bath
I was no where around,
Tried to hide with nary a sound
A hard thing to do
For a chubby and round
Long-eared Bassett hound!

I liked to escape
With an eye for roaming, exploring
 on an adventure all over town
Making it hard to be found

They couldn't decide

the family named Lee
Who was the luckiest
The family or me

If I could vote I would loudly say
it was definitely me
Who was saved from the pound
And they named me Lucky Lee!

With a woof and a wag
You can see
I am one happy puppy
In a family named Lee!

©Joanne Sandlin Benson

Nasar Zulu

A Rhodesian Ridgeback, he was named for a Nazar,
a Turkish eye-shaped amulet to protect against the evil eye.
Nazar means sight, surveillance, attention…and
He emulated all that when he welcomed us home.

His baritone voice, joyous greeting, and wild wagging tail
reminded us he was both a vigilant guard and loving friend.
With eagerness in his bright, warm eyes, he'd seem to say,
"Next time take me with you," or, "Let's go for a walk."

I'd sit with his huge, gentle paw in my hand, and he'd steal
a sloppy lick, a kiss to show he cared. I would stroke his soft
lion-red coat and rough ridged back. I'd peer into penetrating
eyes that looked into my soul and let me glimpse into his.

Nasar lived a full life that many other dogs would envy.
First, going to school and graduating in dog obedience,
then earning the coveted Canine Good Citizen Award.
He had one wife, Nala, and ten stunning Ridgeback pups.
One was a show champion, all of them were beautiful.

Ten years passed quickly, and we humans are too busy.
"In a little while," I'd say. At times too busy for a walk,
or sitting beside him, and then there wasn't another day…
One of the lessons he taught me in his short, precious life.

41

Nasar would rest peacefully on our front porch with Kimba,
his daughter at his side, and we'd gaze at Granite Mountain.
Our hundred-pound African lion dog was ready to go home.
He died under a juniper tree by the gate when we were gone.

Ω
©Sandy Nelson

Kitties

I don't prefer kitties
It's true
They slink;
Leaving hardly a clue.
Appearing quite cute;
So adorable.
But really the devil;
Quite horrible.
Kitties feign friendship,
They do!
But false companions
Asleep on your bed.
Don't die in repose,
They'll chew on your head.
Yes! Really the devil;
Quite horrible.

Ω

©Elizabeth Ajamie-Boyer

©Belisima by Shelley Lowell

Heart to Heart Love

His furry four legs
Caused my heart to beg
For a love so deep
Unknown it could so far creep.

His gorgeous golden face
Caused my life to have space
For a love so amazingly pure
Realizing a forever love-bond beginning to stir.

His unconditional love
Could only have come from above
I longed for his body and heart
And mine to never be apart.
He was named Higgers
A name derived from my birth
He snuggled, played, and kissed slobbers
From his heart to mine with abundant girth.

A joy-filled life that ended at only eleven

But will forever fill me until heaven

To this day his memories instill

A life I longed to be tranquil.

His departure caused my heart to stand still

And ache with an excruciating upheaval

Another would never replace

But would help fill the space

Where pet love needs to embrace.

Ω

©Maureen Wild

My Friend Roy

I go for a walk with my friend Roy
cover some ground at our pace
loves the outdoors just like me
never in a hurry we never race

spreading good cheer along our way
happy with everyone we meet
stay in our neighborhood most of the time
about a mile and our trips complete

cold today the wind was brisk
didn't slow us down at all

out in the morning and afternoon
Roy needs to hear natures call

Roy is my friend my female Pug
she's been with me now for a while
the time we spend together each day
makes me happy it makes me smile

Roy was abused and I adopted her
been 5 months learning about each other
she's doing fine as we journey along
it's me that's on the road to recover

let go of your preconceived normal day
let God work his plan for your joy
it's all up to you to find your way
finding mine with my friend Roy

Ω

©Bruce Sparks

Skylar's Time

His brother then sister no longer here
His time now it was abundantly clear
An only dog-child now he would be
Exclusive attention and love being key.

Heart mourns so deep only room for the one
No more can I do this I adamantly sworn
He vehemently thrived on the exclusive attention
Grew more reclusive and gave over protection.

His dog heart grieved his many losses
His alphas gone and needing his bosses.
My heart hurt not knowing what to do
I loved and I cuddled, disciplined and made due.

Unable to refill his dog heart with more
We both were hurting, empty and forlorn
I needed his love to help fill my voids
Unfair to him we were both depressoids.

At fifteen his body collapsed unable to get up
my heart pierced again with a frenzied club
Said our goodbyes with eyes that understood
Our love for each other truly at magnitude.

My Lord my God graciously gave me a message
A grief-filled devotional to comfort his passage
The excruciating pain of another dog-child gone
A decade would pass before my open heart drawn.

Ω

©Maureen Wild

Little Babette

When my human parents moved away
they did what many people did
with their pets in Baltimore
they abandon them
I was driven to the corner of a city street
about a mile from the harbor
dropped off to fend for myself

My home became the corner storm drain
I ran under parked cars to stay safe
Hid from car and foot traffic

no one knew I was there

I ate leftovers from fast-food wrappers
tossed out of car windows
sometimes I ate cardboard
sometimes I ate plastic wrappers
I hung out in the gutter
always searching for food
I met strays and stood my ground
on rainy days I stayed under parked cars
avoiding the water-drenched storm drain

One summer afternoon
sunning myself in the gutter
next to my storm drain
a big black truck-like car
passed me by and parked
a woman stepped out of it
came over and talked to me
she went in her house
came out with food
I ate everything

she beckoned me to follow her

into her backyard

I did

She gave me more

fresh water and food

I liked her

I stayed for a while

then went back to my drain

The next morning

I heard this woman talking to her dog

they were walking towards my drain

I surfaced and meowed to her

she took her dog home

came back with food

enticed me to her backyard again

This time she picked me up

put me in a carrier and

took me into her house

I met her fur family

this was scary

being in the carrier

I felt safe

Sammy accepted me immediately

Stella was another story

petite about the same size as me

with long black fur like mine

a typical cat-shaped face

same golden-colored eyes as me

her personality unlike me

in every way

she was nasty to me from the start

Winston, oh my God!

a gorgeous card-carrying Persian

beautiful markings

aqua eyes

stunning and gentle-hearted

I melted the moment I saw him

same ancestors

same-shaped face,

same nose, same body build

54

Instant friends

he protected me from Stella

from the start

I had an ally

Stevie was a tuxedo

kind to me from the moment we met

In the morning my new mom

took me for a check-up

with a clean bill of health

I got the official OK

to be part of the family

I stayed and was spayed

I was happy with my new mom

my new family

(not counting Stella)

my new home

a warm bed

good food

but my new name "Muffin"

didn't work for me

My name was Babette

I wanted it back

Mom's shower time was

my time to be alone with her

a chance to have her to myself

during one of our shower times

I laid down on the top of the tub

sending her love

staring into her eyes

we connected telepathically

I sent her my real name

"Babette"

Within seconds she said:

"Babette! That's a lovely name

I think I'll change your name

to Babette"

From then on

she called me Babette

It made me so happy

We had a special connection

that grew and grew

we loved each other

with all our hearts

sixteen beautiful years together

after crossing the rainbow bridge

I still send her my love

Ω

©Shelley Lowell

©Lacy by Shelley Lowell

Bobby

In Edinburg Scotland the tale is told
of a wee graveyard terrier, loyal and bold
Through thick and thin, all seasons ye ken,
they were the best and faithful friends.
John Gray and his sidekick Bobby
Everafter through the end.

John Gray was a watchman
on the streets of Edinburg
"Auld Jock" he was called
All night his good tempered pal
Walked and worked with him
everyone knew
Hey, is that your Bobby
walking with you?

The Dandle Dinmont terrier
scruffy, canny, and nice
survived his master's passing
himself and the graveyard mice.
For when John Gray passed on in 1850
Bobby led the procession into Greyfriars Kirkyard
with the blessings of the city
then sat on his grave unmoving on guard.

As the one o'clock gun shot the blast
from the castle above
Bobby would run for his meal
to John Traill's coffee house
and be treated with love
then straight back to the headstone
where he spent every day of fourteen years
guarding his master alone.

The gardener tried to evict him
as the law directed
but Bobby stayed firm
til his own last days protected
by the good folks in Greyfriars
built a shelter and a headstone
burying Bobby near John
Dog and owner both gone.

To this day Bobby stands

proud and tall in the square

of Candlemaker's Row and George IV Bridge

beneath the bagpipes playing

from the grand castle tall

And for luck passers-by rub the nose of his statue

Never to forget the loyalty

of Bobby, a lesson to us all.

Ω

©Janice Shanks

Engraved on his statue

"Let his loyalty and devotion be a lesson to us all".

©Allens Angel by Shelley Lowell

My Lady

©Pat Fogarty

©Holly by Shelley Lowell

Murph the Mutt

Murph the Mutt is on the prowl,
his belly low, his hind parts high
the war growl rumbling in his throat,
the wrath of dogdom in his eyes.

All you lizards, earthworms, flies,
dragons and other pests, take note
and round the garden raise the cry:
Murph the Mutt is on the prowl.

Ω

©Marilyn Bowden

©Mr. Gray by Shelley Lowell

Ever Curious

ever curious
scoping out who knows what
stand and deliver

Ω

©Judi Armbruster

67

©Trixie by Shelley Lowell

Biology of Dog According to Curly

My *apron*, sweet smell of apricot,
cinnamon and sage
forequarters straight
but weakened with age.

A tight-fisted *flank*
arched with a barreled *keel*
flews don't say much, but persistent
in wanting a meal.

A *muzzle* faithfully searches
for all foreign scents
with *dewlap* hugging collar,
dog tag worth a few cents.

Pasterns once thriving
but now rest on my *rump*
a *stifle* that kicks, and just a dog
always ready for a hump.

69

A proud *prosternum*—

the best of the best

with a *stop* that's superior, highlighting

my lovely prized chest.

I'm Standard Poodle, and you can be sure

I'm loved and adored; pampered, even more.

Ω

© Carole Bolinski

Canine Key:

Apron=chest hair

Forequarters=front section, includes shoulder

blades, upper arms, and forelegs

Flank=the side between the last rib and rear leg

Keel=the lower curve of the chest

Flews=upper lips

Muzzle=protruding area of the face, including nose,

jaw, and mouth

Dewlap=loose skin under the throat and neck

Pasterns=shock-absorbing bones located in the

forelegs and hind legs

Rump=the rear end

Stifle=the knee joint on the back leg

Prosternum=the part of the chest that juts out the

farthest

Stop=where the skull ends toward the muzzle

Ω

©Carole Bolinski

©Lola by Shelley Lowell

A Pet's Prayer

Please let my Love & Loyalty
Remind them, Lord, of You.
And when my final moment comes,
Lord, tell them as we part...
I was a Made-To-Order Gift
From Your great loving Heart

My people are so precious, Lord;
I know You think so too...
And I believe You put me here
To Love them just for You!
They take such gentle care of me
And have such tender hearts...
Please use me, Lord, to comfort them
Whenever teardrops start.
They face a lot of battles
As they live & work each day...
They need me, Lord,
To make them smile
And show them how to play!
The world is full of people,
But sometimes real friends are few...

Ω

©Bruce Sparks

©Pheebee by Shelley Lowell

For Hester

this cat knows something

sitting quietly all day

Ω

©Nellie & Bailey by Shelley Lowell

Dispossessed

When all the horrors
of the world
come seeping
through our windows
and nature's death
comes pounding
at our doors
it seems unfit
for an old landlady
to think
it's life's major dilemma
that an innocent cat
dwell in a sea of love
with no legal lease
©Shelly Lowell

77

©Sebastian by Shelley Lowell

Beautiful Wildflower

A decade passed since her siblings gone
An open heart again was drawn
Daisy, Daisy, my precious wildflower
Mutual abundant love would we fervor

What's a girl to do with a name of Daisy
And a reputation that grew to be fun-loving crazy
Arriving as an only wonder dog-child
And plentifully filled with boundless wild

She came as a rescue to our home
Building a new life song like a poem
Her unending depth of extraordinary love
She rescued us and fit like a glove

Her personality so gentle, submissive, and sweet
To all whom she touches, and loves is a treat
Her trainer expressed an intimate depth of special
That truly deserves some type of medal

Obedient, loving, and agility trained

It's no wonder she'll forever reign

In hearts and lives that need her love

She is a cherished gift from above

Missed loving her brothers and sister non-kin

Everything about her would be a win-win

Human and canine friends abundant are hers

A beautiful life for many more years

Ω

© Maureen Wild

Seamus The Wonder Dog

You always knew
The right thing to do
You raised three kids
And enjoyed it too

I'll never know
If others knew
You were their Guardian Angel
Sent from Heaven above

Your wisdom and fame
Grew and grew

By tales told to other kids

Every day at school

The three children you raised

Who loved you so much

Brought schoolmates to visit

You— Seamus their Wonder Dog

Touted as the dog who never forgets

A kid introduced from school

Like the elephant they say

You never forget

Your memory of those children

Who were introduced to you

Were often tested

By the ignorant few

You growled at strangers

Yet with a wagging tail

Yet greeted those you knew

And maybe gave a lick or two

Your courage and wisdom

Are still told in tales

To the kids and grandkids

Of the kids you knew

Rest in Peace Seamus

Ω

1982 -1996

©Pat Fogarty

©Chaucer by Shelley Lowell

Bugs and the Snake

Bugs has a rock out in the yard
where he likes to go pee
a snake was there and he was aware
so he reported the critter to me

I found the snake in my backyard
and coaxed him into a sack
got him from the desert round here
and I plan to give him back

sidewinder if my vision is right
and dangerous to me and the dog
times like this I wish I had
one a grandpa's rooting hogs

having a hog just to kill critters
ain't worth the time it takes
to feed such a pet and keep him clean
just to keep me out of snakes

so me and Bugs will go for a drive
and turn this rascal loose
Bugs don't mind to take the time
for snakes we got no use

Thanks Bugs
©Bruce Sparks

Oz by Shelley Lowell

My Playmates

My playmates, all through grade school
And into high school years,
They saw me through my happy times,
And wiped away my tears.
They carried no opinions,
They had no angry words,
They merely sat to listen

And to blink at what they heard.

They always came to meet me
No matter day or night
And every time we visited
They always brought delight.
When I, with Mother, spoke harsh things,
Or, with Father, let our voices ring,
Or brother and I had a fight,
My playmates always set me right.
With eyes all bright with sympathy,
And ne'er a word to chastise me,
They came up close, to sniff and purr
To nicker soft, or whine or mew.
And stay 'til I was gone away
To come again another day.

Ω

©Sally Harper Bates

Honeyspot

I was born in the backyard
of a vacant property in Connecticut
my cat dad lived in the house next door.
I looked just like him
his human mom feed my feral family

Cat mama was a stray
I was the sickly runt of the litter
my siblings pushed me away
when I went to nurse or eat
they picked on me

I slept on the side deck
of the vacant house
I wasn't more than 12 weeks
when a lady moved into the house

that evening she came out on the deck
with a small dog much bigger than me
thinking he would attack me
I arched my back and hissed
as loud as I could to scare him off
He ignored me
walked right past me
The next morning

they came out for their morning walk
the moment the door opened
I ran past them into the house

I moved in just like that!
I didn't know five cats
were already living there
AND the dog!

The lady noticed I had my nose
was running
After a trip to a doctor's office
I was put on meds
my life improved
I felt better
got stronger, bigger
slept next to nineteen-year-old Chadwick
who welcomed my presence
played on the bed with the others
they loved my kitten antics
I was entertainment
they treated me fairly, kindly
I had my own bowl
they allowed me to eat
no one pushed me away
I grew up a big strong boy

I was named Honeyspot
my fur, gold and white
a gold "spot" on my white neck
born near Honeyspot Street
my name was a natural

I was the only one in my litter
to escape the wild outdoors
the brutal cold winters
live in a wonderful home
free from fear of predators
surrounded by love
With a cat family
and a dog who accepted me
for who I was

©Shelley Lowell

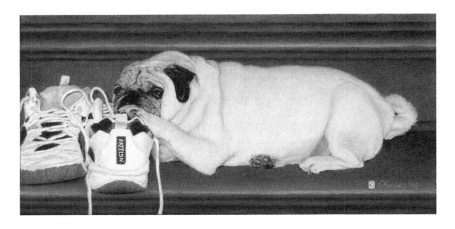

©Dusty by Shelley Lowell

winter fat
bounds my cat
mice are safe

Ω

©Judi Armbruster

©Harry by Shelley Lowell

My New Life

Where I used to live I had a best friend, Laddie.
He died before we moved, so now I'm alone.
Lad and I roamed free on more than an acre.
Now I live in a manufactured home space.
Outside is a tiny place to "do my business."
I'm on a leash when we go for walks,
and my world has shrunk a whole lot.
How do I cope? I bark at people or dogs.
I'm just saying hello, and I mean no harm
But my owners say, "No bark!"
I find a real conflict with that.

As much as I love them, my owners
make noises all day talking to each other,
or to a small thing they hold in their hands.
I think of this as "soft barking."
They soft-bark with other people, but
I'm not allowed to bark-talk with *their* dogs.
Maybe because my bark isn't so soft.
And when evening comes, a black thing
in the living room turns bright, and there are
sounds and "people barking" all evening.

Sometimes, I go out on the deck to get away
from the noise until the bright thing
turns dark again, and I can sleep in peace.
Don't get me wrong. I'm not complaining.
I went to the "humane place" for a dog class
and heard all the lonely dogs crying in cages.

There are places where one can't have a dog.
Imagine that? Dogs always want people.
So, I'm happy where I am and well-loved.
I gaze up at them with my dark brown,
obedient eyes, and do not bark.

Ω

©Sandy Nelson

Growling *Gato*

No meows from Como-no indeed.
Sheared for the summer heat Como growls.
When catnapping Como growls not purrs.
Como might be mistaken for a feral cat;
rather than a stray or abused kitten rescue.

In the shelter, Como sat distanced from other cats.
Rather royal and splendid in a fluffy gray-white coat.
Once home, Como shot straight up into the air,
chased around the house then hid under a bed growling.
No gentle pets, snuggles or loving meows-just growls.

Persistent gentle coaxing and a bribe of milk
ushered a softer growl while gobbling like a pig.
A virgin voyager as a cat owner, I was bewildered.
Time, patience and persistent purrs on my part
hoped to induce meows rather than growls by Como.

Time appears to heal all wounds and slowly Como
and our relationship grew where he walked
the mountain by my side growling at one spot in the
orchard.
Recovering from gut surgery, Como kneaded my
stomach.
Not only was he a protector but maybe a nurse cat.

An outside guy, clearing the area of birds, rats and
squirrels,
Como fought fiercely with raccoons on the property but
dodged
wolves and deer that frequented our Montana acreage.
As sentry and guard, Como lavished his role in the
outdoors.
Como, an unusual *gato,* remained to growl and not *miau.*
Ω

© Dolores Comeaux-Everard

Hi, I'm Kenzi!

Seven and a half pounds—that's all
Not even close to a bowling ball.
A "foster failure." That's what they call me
How can you fail with a new family?
I was born in Indiana, a Hoosier pooch
So irresistible you can't help but smooch.
My mom loves dogs. She fostered 100
How can I let her go? She wondered.

Mom gave me my name and an Indiana home

But then off to Arizona we roamed.

Watch out for the coyotes, owls and hawks

I'm always leashed whenever we walk.

She entered me in a cute dog contest.

To the winner, tickets for a game with the Suns

Got enough votes and guess what, we won!

So who went? Mom and Dad.

Still, I wasn't so sad.

I've got folks who care about little old me

The foster failure, a proud part of the "we."

Ω

©Dennis Royalty

Spud

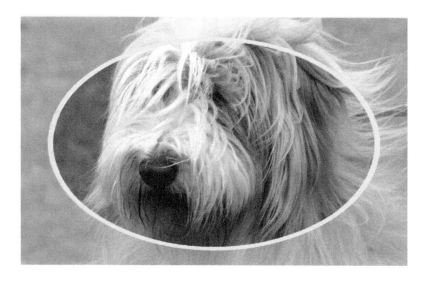

growing up the way I did, was the best that I could do
never feeling unloved at all, having family as I grew
every day was endless wonder, my dog was there with me
we always had great adventures, and exciting things to see
time went past the days stretched on, I found as I got bigger
in that time as Spud got older, he began to lose his vigor
he didn't run and jump as well, and laid a around a lot
seemed he got tired quicker, couldn't run just barely trot
came the day he wouldn't get up, he just didn't want to
within a few days he was gone, wasn't nothing I could do
on the desert, outside of town, I found a place with shade
buried Spud with honor and grace, his memory will never
fade
I look back on the times we had, together in the sun
my pal, my best friend, there'll never be another one

all the years since I lost my friend, I remember times to tell

my first love in all this world, was that old dog I knew so well

Ω

©Bruce Sparks

Bo's Song

A step-dog she would be

As her dad and I committed to marry

My two boys and she a girl

All three--let's give it a whirl

As we blended our new family.

Their living spaces so different
We'd have to define how to complement
Full reign access versus only outside
Making decisions on how dogs reside.

To me, more than just a dog
To him, just a pet
A need for some special sweet talk
And for him a heart-mind reset.

She was so sweet I missed her inside
But in her yard was all she knew
Time with her was met outside
In those moments our bond grew.

She filled the girl-void I never had
Bringing connections her dog heart glad
She would hop and run and bring delight
Sealing our relationship as love airtight.

A move from Mesa to Washington state
Brought major changes and a mess in a crate
At sixteen she made this move

Little did we know her dog spirit improve.

The years vanished as she became like a pup
Loving the new climate, wet, rain and snow
Plus indoor space which gave her some pep
Caused us to notice and exclaim with a "Whoa!"

She loved her new life despite aging bones
We never heard her elderly groans
I held her close until almost eighteen
With cherished memories of abundance serene.

Ω

©Maureen Wild

©Hogan by Shelley Lowell

Buttons a/k/a Muffin Girl

When I was born
my umbilical cord wrapped
around my left rear foot
amputating it
my breeder
thinking I was male
and unbreedable
took me to her vet
to send me over
the rainbow bridge

The vet refused

A woman called
wanting a Himalayan cat
I was the last of my litter
not very adoptable
due to my leg

The moment
this woman saw me
it was love at first sight

she didn't care I limped

or had a short leg

She adopted me

took me to her vet

to make sure

I was healthy

the vet looked

and looked

and looked

at my little bottom

Finally my new mom asked

what's the matter?

He said

this cat is healthy but "he" is a "she".

my mom didn't care what my sex was

she was happy I was healthy

We came home

mom called the breeder

letting her know I was healthy

and that "he" was a "she".

The breeder wanted me back

she could breed a female

my mom refused

I heard her say

no female cat with a short leg

is going to hobble around

carrying kittens

no way!

I was relieved

mom protected me

we were inseparable

I was such a little fur ball

she carried me around

the house in her sweater

it served as a pouch

I felt like a baby kangaroo

Soon she noticed

something wasn't right

I was in pain

we went back to the vet

I was running a high fever

he didn't know its cause

Maybe it's her foot
mom suggested

He replied
most animals don't run
a high fever because of pain
maybe it wasn't a clean break
there could be an infection

Once he cleaned the area
around the break
my temperature
dropped to normal
I was free from pain
happier
comfortable
thriving

I thumped around
on my 3 and a half legs
climbing chair backs
with my front legs
compensating, adjusting

to my so-called handicap

with ease and grace

I lived to the ripe old age of 19

giving my mom much joy and love

she gave it back to me in buckets

After I crossed the rainbow bridge

she adopted 2 cats to fill

the hole I left in her heart

Ω

©Shelley Lowell

©Sammy and Stevie by Shelley Lowell

Rodeo and the Coyotes

By night they descend from the hills.
Hunger drives them
Prowling through the arroyo
Behind walled properties,
Beneath the eyes of the moon.

They reconnoiter, forage for morsels,
Sleeping rabbits, stray cats, refuse.
Listen! They howl to the heavens in chorus.
Strident primordial yelps.
Ever louder, ever closer,
Until the commotion lodges
Directly behind our wall.

The German shepherd rouses,
Rises to all fours, ears erect.
Mane bristling, he leaps for the door.
With a guttural growl,
He paws at the glass,
Demands to get out, get to them.

"No, Rodeo, stay, boy, stay!"

Listen! The chorus has transformed

To high-pitched whines and barks.

The pack beckons Rodeo to join them.

"Come on, pal. We're a bunch of fellow dogs".

Rodeo knows better. But he's a fighter.

Wants to take them on.

"Rodeo, stay! They outnumber you, Rode."

Rodeo heeds, pivots a tight circle

By the fireplace and reluctantly lies down,

Still snarling. The coyotes lose patience.

Their howls resume, then gradually recede.

Pickings may be better elsewhere.

©Ernest Griffith

My Sand

Fierce Vigilant Fearless

All with the same goal

Protecting my sand is their objective

Be it rain sleet or snow

These three canines

Will never leave their post

Unless perchance you possess

An ample supply of canine treats

Or maybe if they see a rabbit flee

My keen-eyed puppy taunts her prissy

Pinscher tutor to surprise pounces

While her patient teacher ignores her growls

While in the rear in the comfort of the cab

The older Irish Terrier watches as

Miss Regal Dobermann ignors the pup

As the years passed

And the more sand I hauled

My three Fierce, Fearless & Vigilant Friends

Never failed to Guard & Protect

My Sand

Ω

©Pat Fogarty

Ode to Smokey and Sabrina

Some dogs are spoiled, some dogs are haughty,
Then there are dogs who are just plain naughty.

Our rescue Lab mix, and our purebred Bichon,
Were too much to handle for dog trainer Ron.

No fence, no pen, could them contain,
Escape from jail was their best game.

For them our yard was just too small,
The open country sang its call.

Rattlesnakes and porcupines near and far,
Financed our veterinarian's new car.

Their life of crime would one day end,

The dogcatcher was not their friend.

I think that Rufus was his name.
He was no doofus at his game.

Mulberry Lane, a mile away,
Was their playground one Winter day.

The trash cans offered too much fun,
They tipped them over, one by one.

Returning home without a care,
Rufus followed them to their lair.

And on our door, he did mount,
His summons with one serious count.

"Dogs at Large" were we entrusted;
Our delinquent dogs had gotten busted.

To ensure that justice surely prevailed,
Rufus described the dogs to be jailed.

His dog-breed knowledge was sorely lacking,
But close enough to send us packing.

"Black Labrador with white spot on its chest,

And small white Poodle with red sweater vest."
The story has a happy end.
We never heard from Rufus again.

I suspect he was content to know,
He had chastised us with one mighty blow.

We loved those dogs, despite their crimes,
And they returned that love a thousand times.

©Jim Downey

©Nico and Bijou. By Shelley Lowell

Old Tom

laying on our back porch, cut up, scarred, patches of hair
missing blood caked fur, beaten and battered, not in the
mood for kissing

big yellow tom, been out catting around, home now from
the war
don't know why he fights, vying for ladies, a need to
settle a score

dad checks him for need of a vet, some wounds are still
bleeding
says he'll heal, not much we can do, a week or two he's
needing

soon he'll be healing, and stronger feeling, getting just
about right
off he'll go to roam, leaving his good home, looking for a
fight

seems to be his goal fore he gets too old
to be the all around king loving ladies,
off acting shady, fighting for the title is the thing

when he was small he was cute and cuddly I picked a
name to fit
came up with sweet Tootsie Roll, but I reckon he grew
out of it

Old Tom ain't no house cat, he's going places spreading
his seed
I guess the Good Lord, with wisdom, made the old tom to
breed

I felt a good deal of responsibility for the way he lived
his life
might have turned out different if the old bastard had him
a wife

some years later Old Tom left home and never ever did
come back
reckon he met with another old tom and got himself
bushwhacked

kitties grow into cats, some are cute, but surely some that
ain't
my little kitty Tootsie Roll, Old Tom, was a bonafide
fighting saint.

Ω

©Bruce Sparks

Nash

Could it Be
Synchronicity speaks
The teacher appears
When the student seeks
It all started with a chance encounter
Joanne and I stopped at the counter
For coffee and tea when
I looked around and found two seats
We sat and talked of daily deeds
Without a thought of privacy
When a stranger approached
and said to my bride and me
Pardon me folks I could not help but hear
Sound like you two share a trait with me
In my mind I thought, what could it be
I know a few nuts visit here
And that's when she said
Your Love of animals
Is clear to me
So I asked her to have a seat
We talked and talked and after a call
Joanne and I agreed to see
Her charge of Cats
She tended for free.

So right next door a pet store be
And after some forms were filled
I volunteered
To help for free
The joy comfort and tender love
I saw in their eyes
And they in mine
Will stay in my Heart
Til the end of time
Ω

©Frank Bosco

Kitteh Rap

Mostly he be sleepin

You know he chillin,

But da mouses be weepin

When he get to killin

He show no mercy to a lizard or a sparrow

He on them critters fasta than a arrow

Kitteh ain't neva gon' lose his cool

You waitin for dat, den you da fool!

Cheh cheh cheh cheh cheh meow meow

Kitteh kitteh kitteh here he come now

Look out suckas, he own da place

Look out suckas, he gon' sleep on yo face

He know how to play you when he start to purr

He know how to get you pettin his fur

Cheh cheh cheh cheh cheh meow meow

Kitteh kitteh kitteh here he come now

Try rubbin his belly or clippin his claws

You gon' find out quick how much blood he draws

He nuthin but a four-legged murder machine

But the cutest damn thing you ever seen

Cheh cheh cheh cheh cheh meow meow

Kitteh kitteh kitteh here he come now

Ω

©Mark Wenden

An Hour Later

That big metal food truck

Put away for the day

Daddy walks away

The door is closed

I'm no fool

I smell the food

I am a dog

Separated by that door

This pup is ready to sup

Separated by that door

Then the gust

Leads to my lust

That door swung open

And the bags were opened

General Tso and howl

Oh lookie

Fortune cookies

So much to eat

What a treat

Mommy's home and turn pale

I'm so full

I can't move 'cept wag my tail

My tummy's better

My Vet's not too upset

He just wanted to know

Was I hungry an hour later

Ω

©Maureen Norcross

Winston

Sue and Ben adopted me
when they were a couple
after he broke up with Sue
I went to live with him
Life was good until
he had to go to war
Sue promised to care for me
while he was away
That didn't work out
she took her anger out
on me for their break up
she developed a cat allergy
I was never touched
picked up
kissed or
hugged again
I was miserable
I missed my dad
I overheard Sue bitterly
complain about me
to all she knew
I missed affection
nothing I did pleased her
I ran away twice
twice she found me

129

One day she put me in a carrier
took me to her workplace
a woman in her office
heard about me
offered to foster me
until dad came back
I was nervous, scared
uncertain of what
would happen to me
once in her home
she picked me up
hugged me
held me in her arms
kissed me
petted me
gave me a big dinner
introduced me to Chadwick
my new brother
my new best buddy
we napped together
back to back
spending our days together
while our mom was at work
I was so happy
all the hugging
loving
caring

I now received
made up for those
sad years of neglect
Finally content
I never thought about
running away again

Ω

©Shellley Lowell

©Mr. Gray Small by Shelley Lowell

Writing a Poem about Toby

If I could write a poem about my dog,
I would say he's been the greatest joy and best
friend in my life.
He's been the most unconditional loving partner
I've ever had.

If I could write a poem about my dog,

the words would shine,

the pen would be bright gold,

the paper would be the most expensive paper I
could buy.

If I could write a poem about my dog,

I'd hold it to my heart,

I'd kiss it gently,

and I'd put it on my altar

for the rest of my days.

Ω

©Kaya Kotzen

Skippy And Pablo

We had a little puppy
When I was a tot, so wee
We called him Skippy
So much for creativity!

At first it was just
Peter and me
Then, Tom was born
And we became three

Living four stories up
Without an elevator
Having a puppy
For Mom, was the deal breaker

She decided to give him
To a boy named Pablo
He lived across from Grandma
A basement apartment in the Barrio

Mom said we would still see him
When we walked over to University
To visit Grandma
Way back in 1953

I remember crying
Tears running down my face

As we waved goodbye to Skippy
And Pablo took our place

Then, one day we moved
Right next door to Grandma
But, Pablo had moved away too
I cried again for Skippy was no more.

I would never allow myself
To get close to an animal again
This little boy's pain was deep
Having twice lost my furry friend.

The years rolled on by
And we adopted another pet
A shepherd that we named Smokey
He was really the best

But memories deep within me
Wouldn't let me love him the way I should
Even though he was a member
Of the 'Doyle Brotherhood'

Dad would get pissed at one of us
And scream the roster of our names
Peter, Michael, Smokey, Chris!
'Dammit' he say... he forgot Tom again!

Now that I'm a man
And in my Seventies

Still fearful of surrendering to love
Tho, I do it ever so cautiously

We are now Cat-Dads
To four wonderful kitties
When I whisper in their ears
'Do you know how much I love you?'
It is a true love...
Shadowed by childhood fears

I know someday we will lose them
But, not to Pablo this time
When they cross the Rainbow Bridge
I will be thankful that they were mine.

Ω

©Mike Doyle

Digital Art "Old Blue Eyes" ©Pat Fogarty

Cocoa

My human parent was ill
no one was caring for me
someone opened
the front door
I ran out
down concrete steps
to find my new home

I crossed the yard
towards a house
I was grabbed
from behind
swooped up
put in a box
taken to a place
where cats sleep
in wired cages

People came by
looked at us
some of us

were taken out

hugged

cuddled

put back

others never

came back

I wished someone

would hug me

take me home

A woman stopped

at my cage

I was taken out

hugged

cuddled

I felt so loved

I wanted to stay

In her arms

forever

I was put back

A day later

she came back

hugged me

kissed my head

cradled me

In her arms

took me home

I found my new home!

I was fed yummy

healthy food

given lots of

affection

I met two cats

that looked like me

they were

my new brother

my new sister

One happy family

Soon my new mom

noticed I had a problem

She took me
to doctor
after doctor
after doctor
I got tests
after tests
after tests
the cause of
my discomfort
couldn't be found

I wanted to be
with my new mom
forever

I got sicker
and sicker
I was finally
diagnosed with
a liver shunt

Protein
from my food
was poisoning
my body
it was too late
nothing
could be done

Two months
with my new mom
was my best time
on earth
I wished I could be
with her forever

She helped me over
the rainbow bridge
where I would
feel good again
she was with me
to the end of
my earthly life

I am with her now

she can't see me

she carries me

in her heart

Ω

©Shelly Lowel

Roy Boy

My eyes cry every night
for you my sweet friend
my heart is shattered
I miss you I miss you I miss you

I miss holding you
I miss seeing you sleep

145

I miss watching you eat

And I miss you watching me

Without you my furry friend

Life is not the same

Nor will it ever be

And now I struggle every day

Yet when I sleep and

When I dream

I know

You are and will always be

A part of me that

No one sees

Someday over the Rainbow

We will be together forever

When it's my turn to cross

Over the heavenly rainbow bridge.

Ω

©Frank Bosco

Faithful One

He arrived as a rescue
Needing a brother
His personality grew
As I added another.

Fluffy, black with tips of white
His playful smile shined exuberant bright
He loved his new golden brother
Each one smothered the other.

Once named Tripper
But something better needed to capture
His faithfulness made him a Cisco
And his heart love abundant on turbo.

Never understanding his fifty-pound size
As he jockeyed and snuggled for the prize
A time to cuddle on momma's lap
One of the best places for a good long nap.

He grieved his brother's loss
A love so deep and apparent life-force

He bonded quickly to another
A puppy this time he'd gratefully surrender.

His fourteen years ended too abruptly
A heart problem diagnosed way too suddenly
Momma's goodbye was extremely painful
As he cuddled to the end amazingly faithful.

Ω

©Maureen Wild

My Pandemic Cat

loves that I've been home so much

during the pandemic. He has me all

to himself, it's like we're roommates.

I ask about his plans for the day, but

planning isn't in his wheelhouse. Mostly

he naps or does yoga with me, attends

zooms with me. He seems to like

my zoom buddies. Sometimes I read

my poems to him and he purrs loudly,

thrums like a little engine. I see him

in a different light than before Covid,

we're more connected, at similar levels

of existence. He can tell when I'm lonely,

plops his furry self on my lap. It's nice

to have a living being to say I love you

to. Tonight, we're watching reruns of

Breaking Bad.

Ω

© Roxanne Doty

Springtime Snow

A Sunday Springtime Snow Shower
Fell in little tufts of fluff
I know that my friends back East
Have had more than enough!
I took my Cat named Jax
And we went out back
He loves the snowflakes on his face
As long as he's secure
In my Cat-Dad embrace
As the floaty powdery flakes
Fell from on high
Darkness had descended upon us
From the night sky
The universe was ours
You couldn't hear a sound
As far as I could tell
Not another soul around
Perfect little moments like this
Are refreshing to my soul
A few minutes of absolute serenity
You don't even notice the cold
Our little time of respite

Was only five minutes long
Then we went back inside
To get all toasty warm
I bid goodnight to the beauty outdoors
Rob had the fireplace lit
Three more cats cozily napping
On a comfy old sofa I would sit
And I smiled to myself
Thinking how much
I love the beauty
In life's simple stuff
Ω

©Mike Doyle

Go Fish!

I'm Stryder, a huge black lab. My owners call me Big Shot.

They're my family, husband and wife, and they like me a lot.

Now, I'm a fisherman on the Russian River, believe it or not!

One day at the river, not far from the ranch, I caught a trout.

I was so proud that I brought it to them, flopping in my mouth.

They were stunned that I'd carried the fish home in my snout.

After that, when we went to the river they'd tell me, "Go fish!"

I tried my best because catching one more was my greatest wish.
It didn't happen, though I'd fish until the water turned blackish.

Our rustic cabin had an ancient porch outside the front door.
One day I was chasing lizards under the steps, loving the chore.
My owners left saying, "Big Shot, go fish!" Asking once more!

When they came home hours later, I showed them what I'd done.
The old redwood porch was torn apart, no steps left, not even one...
I held a dead lizard in my mouth, displaying my newfound fun.

Frowning, they didn't scold me, so I relaxed and stared up at them.
They smiled and all I can say is they never asked me to go fish again.

Ω

©Sandy Nelson

My Cat

Warmth across my chest,

loving snuggles.

He seems to know when

...to just be.

He lays down by me, not able to speak,

but seems to know what just to say.

He does not judge,

he is just him.

He loves me in his own way.

©Christina Lynn

©Sam by Shelley Lowell

Elektra Cat

Elektra Cat was golden and shiny;

She dashes about with the zoomies!

Brightening a room into all the dark corners;

She chases away all the gloomies!

We dearly love our Elektra Cat;

You'd think we are quite taken.

If ever she left us, I want you to know,

We'd all be totally shaken!

©Elizabeth Ajamie-Boyer

©Buddy by Shelley Lowell

Willow Lake

You were and are the face of God, my loyal friend

I take you everywhere now as I did when you lived.

I came here today to face a favorite spot without you.

You loved the ride here, the feel of the wind here,

the smell of pine here beneath the shade of trees

with rocks everywhere

This was one of our favorite spots here.

You would lounge, I would write, then we would walk the waters' edge.

There was a time you would put more than your toes in the water,

when you would swim and play fetch the stick

You romped and leaped and I waded in beside you.

In lake Michigan when you were younger,

you bounded in like a jumping rabbit

Not as much in later years, but the water was still fun

for you and I both.

Today, I sit without you here and remember those days well.

I've been painting your picture here, from a photo

in art class

working slowly and patiently to make you look like

yourself

I wasn't ready to face this place until now.

The winds still blow a little fierce today and the

ripples of water

roll on but you are not here beside me.

Surely, you watch it from wherever you are

and you can swim and leap and bound again if you

choose

Me, I continue to age without you, steadily,

and with more wisdom and grace than I have ever

known.

Grateful for this, my next phase filled with travel,

yet missing your lop-eared smile and smell

waking me up in the morning or coming in to see

me

as I sit on the toilet or in the bathtub.

I miss your crossed paws sitting position, most of

all.

You were such a gentle soul in that pose, taking it
all in.

Instead, I watch a shepherd sitting in the lake,

enjoying the cold and I watch others walking their
dogs

around the rocks on the shore

I remember it all, the times we spent here,

but today is a different time.

I came here to write, to remember, and reflect,

and maybe kayak if the winds die down.

The shepherd turns his head and faces me, his body
still in

the water, ears standing tall.

I see a paddle-boarder on the water on bended
knees,

too unsteady yet to stand.

I can't help myself. I must say hello to the shepherd

He's in his prime and reminds me of the one I
loved.

Toby, are you watching?

The winds blow all around me, and they heal me
even now.

Toby, you are a part of the ripples on the water,

having been spread on a forest floor somewhere,

your ashes long since dispersed.

You are all around me everywhere,

my joy and blessing, guardian angel forevermore.

Ω

©Kaya Kotzen

Wishful Thinking

*The most magical things can happen
and it starts with a wish-Pinocchio*

Pets real and imagined—calm, comfort, and console
except elephants and dolphins, a bit too large to cuddle.
Both familiars, supernatural entities, assist me as
helpmates.
Clinging to a toy elephant as a child cinched my belief

in familiars and guardian angels throughout my life.

Elephants are good role models for living and loving.

Loyal to the core with sensitive trunks that trumpet calls

communicating through vibrations and body language.

Tough skin helps cool them down as they eat the day away.

Elephants never forget which aids and abets senior moments.
Dolphins with perpetual smiles and playful natures
enhance joy and glee within family groups of strong bonds.
Living in Galveston across the street from the ocean
Dolphin-love bloomed watching them chase, throw
seaweed
and leap toward the sky forming a heart mid-air.

The most magical things can happen…
Ω
© DOLORES COMEAUX-EVERARD

Thank You for reading our *Poems of Cats and Dogs*
I have one small request.

If you or someone you know are thinking of bringing a cat or a dog into your home, please visit your local animal shelter and see if one of their adorable and adoptable pets fits your needs

One last thing; before collecting poems for this anthology, I had no idea that some pet stores across the country work hand and hand with animal shelters to find homes for cats and dogs who otherwise would not have much of a chance to find a forever home.

One of the poets, Frank Bosco, told me his story about how he, as a volunteer, worked with rescue animals at Petsmart. Frank was trained by PetSmart personnel and other volunteers on how to work with a stray or a feral animal to be readied for adoption. Frank eventually adopted a feral cat that he had worked patiently with for months. That feral cat and hundreds of other animals in the same situation would never have found that forever home without the caring volunteers and animal rescue organizations working with commercial pet stores across the USA.

Just one of the many great cover design suggestions submitted.

This striking cover was submitted by Artist, Graphic Designer, and Poet Shelley Lowell.

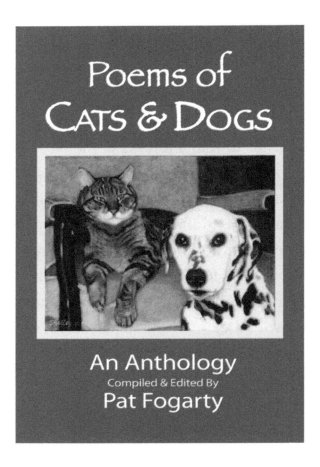

End Notes

Renowned Artist Shelley Lowell allowed us to use some of her paintings of Cats & Dogs in this collection.

Just so you know, I placed one of her paintings on even-numbered pages that would have been blank had I not used her awesome paintings.

I would like to express my gratitude to Shelley Lowell for permitting me to use her copyrighted work to make this collection a more enjoyable anthology of Cat & Dog Poems

Shelley's Contact information is below.

Cat and Dog paintings by Shelley Lowell.
Shelley paints portraits of pets and people on a commissioned basis and has been doing so since 1999.

For more information, visit www.greatpetpaintings.com
shelleyartist143@gmail.com
Prescott Valley, AZ
203.628.5355

Made in the USA
Columbia, SC
21 April 2023